# First World War
and Army of Occupation
## War Diary
France, Belgium and Germany

29 DIVISION
Divisional Troops
16 Sanitary Section
12 April 1916 - 31 March 1917

WO95/2297/2

The Naval & Military Press Ltd
www.nmarchive.com
**Published in association with The National Archives**

Published by

## The Naval & Military Press Ltd

Unit 10 Ridgewood Industrial Park,

Uckfield, East Sussex,

TN22 5QE England

Tel: +44 (0) 1825 749494

www.naval-military-press.com

www.nmarchive.com

*This diary has been reprinted in facsimile from the original. Any imperfections are inevitably reproduced and the quality may fall short of modern type and cartographic standards.*

© **Crown Copyright**
**Images reproduced by permission of The National Archives, London, England, 2015.**

# Contents

| Document type | Place/Title | Date From | Date To |
|---|---|---|---|
| Heading | WO95/2297-2 | | |
| Heading | 29th Division Medical No. 16 Sanitary Section Apr 1916- March 1917 To 4 Army. | | |
| Heading | No. 16 Sanitary Sections April-May 1916 | | |
| War Diary | Acheux Somme France | 12/04/1916 | 31/05/1916 |
| War Diary | | 21/05/1916 | 28/05/1916 |
| War Diary | Acheux Somme France | 30/04/1916 | 31/05/1916 |
| War Diary | War Diary of 16th Sanitary Section 12.4.16 to 31.7.16 Volume 21 to 24. July 1916. | | |
| War Diary | Acheux Somme France | 06/06/1916 | 08/07/1916 |
| War Diary | Acheux | 09/07/1916 | 28/07/1916 |
| War Diary | Poperinghe | 29/07/1916 | 31/07/1916 |
| Diagram etc | 16th San Section. | | |
| Diagram etc | 16th San. Sectn. Latrine & Urine Pit | | |
| Diagram etc | Singleton 16th San Sect. | | |
| Diagram etc | Wood 16th San. Sect. Incinerator. | | |
| Diagram etc | 16th San Sect. | | |
| War Diary | 16th San. Sect Greave Trace for Kitchen Sullage | | |
| Heading | War Diary of O.C. 16th Sanitary Section R.A.M.C. C.F. From 1st to 31st August 1916 (Volume 25.) | | |
| War Diary | Poperinghe | 01/08/1916 | 31/08/1916 |
| Heading | War Diary of Sanitary Section 16 R.A.M.C.T. from Sep. 1- Sep. 30 1916 Volume No 26. | | |
| War Diary | Poperinghe | 01/09/1916 | 30/09/1916 |
| Heading | 29th Div. 16th Sanitary Section. Oct 1916. | | |
| Heading | War Diary Sanitary Section 16 (29th Divn) R.A.M.C.T. No. 20. Vol 7. | | |
| War Diary | Poperinghe | 01/10/1916 | 06/10/1916 |
| War Diary | Corbie | 07/10/1916 | 10/10/1916 |
| War Diary | Ribemont | 11/10/1916 | 19/10/1916 |
| War Diary | E 11 Central Camp. | 20/10/1916 | 30/10/1916 |
| War Diary | Corbie | 31/10/1916 | 31/10/1916 |
| Heading | War Diary Sanitary Section 16 R A M C T November 1916 No. 28. Vol 8. | | |
| War Diary | Corbie | 01/11/1916 | 16/11/1916 |
| War Diary | A.2.d.9.7. | 17/11/1916 | 30/11/1916 |
| Heading | War Diary Sanitary Section 16 R.A.M.C. T.F. Vol 9. | | |
| War Diary | A.2.d.9.7. | 01/12/1916 | 11/12/1916 |
| War Diary | Meaulte | 12/12/1916 | 12/12/1916 |
| War Diary | Riencourt | 13/12/1916 | 31/12/1916 |
| Heading | War Diary Sanitary Section 16 R.A.M.C.T. No. 23. Vol 10. | | |
| Miscellaneous | A.D.M.S. 29th. Division No. R.315/3. | 12/02/1917 | 12/02/1917 |
| War Diary | Riencourt | 01/01/1917 | 10/01/1917 |
| War Diary | Corbie | 11/01/1917 | 15/01/1917 |
| War Diary | A.2.d.9.7 | 16/01/1917 | 31/01/1917 |
| Heading | War Diary Sanitary Section 16 R.A.M.C.T. No 24 Vol XI. | | |
| War Diary | Carnoy A.2.d.9.7. | 01/02/1917 | 07/02/1917 |
| War Diary | Heilly | 08/02/1917 | 20/02/1917 |

| | | | |
|---|---|---|---|
| War Diary | Minden Post. | 21/02/1917 | 28/02/1917 |
| Heading | War Diary Sanitary Section 16 R.A.M.C.T. March 1917 No 25. Vol 12. | | |
| War Diary | Minden Post | 01/03/1917 | 03/03/1917 |
| War Diary | Heilly | 04/03/1917 | 19/03/1917 |
| War Diary | Riencourt | 20/03/1917 | 29/03/1917 |
| War Diary | Vignacourt | 30/03/1917 | 31/03/1917 |

Moas/229u/2

29TH DIVISION
MEDICAL

NO. 16 SANITARY SECTION
APR 1916 – MARCH 1917

To 4 ARMY

No. 16 Sundary Letters

**Army Form C. 2118**

# WAR DIARY
## of 16th Sanitary Section, 29th Division
### INTELLIGENCE SUMMARY
*(Erase heading not required.)*

L. Wade Surg Capt. R.A.M.C. Sect.

| Place | Date | Hour | Summary of Events and Information | Remarks and references to Appendices |
|---|---|---|---|---|
| Acheux Somme France | April 1916 | | Assumed command 16th Sanitary Section | |
| | 13.4.16 | | & inspected Visited Engelbelmer & Mailly-Maillet on horseback | |
| | 14.4.16 | | Visited & inspected Louvencourt & Vauchelles. Inspected Acheux two villages where the Engineers task establishing. Interviewed C.R.E. re water supply & purification of wells. Interviewed Medical Officers in Engelbelmer & Mailly-Maillet re improvement of sanitary conditions | |
| | 15.4.16 | | The billets in villages in Divisional area were found very dirty, in some cases men had defaecated freely in corners & on floor of their sleeping places. Large quantities of old rubbish (including some sort of French uniforms) were found in & about billets lately having been used by previous English & French troops. Sanitary Section Motor lorry reported & was taken on establishment. Formed conclusion that to maintain sanitary conditions of village & camp areas sanitary labour beyond that supplied by the units & wrote to A.D.M.S. suggesting that 105 P.B. men should be sent from Base to allot one for Sanitary & Public Health duties to the different villages & camp areas in the Division | |

# WAR DIARY or INTELLIGENCE SUMMARY

Army Form C. 2118

(Erase heading not required.)

| Place | Date | Hour | Summary of Events and Information | Remarks and references to Appendices |
|---|---|---|---|---|
| Advanced, Somme, France | 16.4.16 | | Visited & inspected Beauquesne, Raincheval, Louvencourt & Anquesnes. Distributed men of Sanitary Section in the villages of Divison which are Louvencourt, Anquesnes, Raincheval, Acheux, Mailly-Maillet, Englebelmer & Auchonvillers, Beaucourt. Raincheval had never been totally swept in, neglected order of 16th R.I.R. No men billeted in Auchonvillers but to reverse his transfer & had cases done by affected from Mailly-Maillet. A.L/c attached to H.Q. of Division by request of A.D.C.I. Made out Duties of N.C.O.s in Carl-r billets, written circulated to N.C.O.s & N.D.M.S | |
| | 17.4.16 | | Interviewed C.R.E. re water supply arranged for tests of all wells. Drew Riding Horse from Mobile Vet. Section (took it to stables at Aux). Prepared scheme of report to be used by N.C.O.s in villages &c acted weekly & of routine & of D.R.L.S. digest. Prepared plan for erection of latrines in villages to occupy a part of billets. Visited Auchonvillers, left orders to Divisional front line. Arranged for fatigue parties to [...] clean up Auchonvillers. Interviewed D.R.O.s re Sanitation of front line. | |
| | 19.4.16 | | Inspected Acheux. Lieutenants & reports from district which allows poor efficiency of latrines supplies, pails, incinerators & urinals. Water Supply all irregularly studied. Made stops recommendations on those that [...] | L.F.S. |

Army Form C. 2118

# WAR DIARY 16 Sanitary Section
## or
## INTELLIGENCE SUMMARY
*(Erase heading not required.)*

Instructions regarding War Diaries and Intelligence Summaries are contained in F.S. Regs., Part II. and the Staff Manual respectively. Title Pages will be prepared in manuscript.

| Place | Date | Hour | Summary of Events and Information | Remarks and references to Appendices |
|---|---|---|---|---|
| Achiex Somme France | 20.4.16 | | Conference at Achiex with Messrs Liaison Officer Claus, Spring Division. Entered details re sanitary conditions. Maine agrees to all cleaning up of manure. | |
| | 21.5.16 | | Public latrines begun at Achiex. Sanitary material distributed in McCaren to Dilbey in Division. Inspector Achiex (in French) Wrote notice re manure to habitats of village. Visited Argüens | |
| | 22.5.16 | | Puyelechée, Henly, Auchonvillers. | |
| | 23.5.16 | | Inspected Achiex. Visited Sourencourt & Argüens. Water tested at Achiex & Sourencourt. | |
| | 24.5.16 | | Route village inspection. Water tests Argüens, Puyelechée, Henly | |
| | 25.5.16 | | " " | |
| | 26.5.16 | | " Visited H.Q. 8th "Corps" + handed D.D.M.S. | Plan of Animals Rhodes |
| | 27.5.16 | | Achiex. Plan of new incinerator. Route village inspection & visit further. Report on all wells in area sent to A.D.M.S. | |
| | 28.5.16 | | Visit. Saw Report sent to A.D.M.S. Route village inspection & also visit to Mairie to inspect dump on line along Mairie Auchonvillers light railway. Got lorry at Englebelmer Auchonvillers to help forward loads | Monthly Report appended |

# WAR DIARY
## INTELLIGENCE SUMMARY

Army Form C. 2118

of 1/6 Sanitary Section, 29th Division

*(Erase heading not required.)*

| Place | Date | Hour | Summary of Events and Information | Remarks and references to Appendices |
|---|---|---|---|---|
| Acheux, Somme, France | 29.4.16 | | Special inspection Sucrerie Water Supply & water cart filling at Puchevic. Routine Sanitary inspection. | Settlers made of all cellars made & kept carefully aero. Cellars cleared of litter. Inhabitants once cautioned for slight uses. Where this is an additive there the inhabitants to be notified. |
| | 30.4.16 | | Nch. Rest & preparing road construction for Div.? | |
| | May 1 16 | | Routine Village inspection. Plan made for disposal of Batt. Waste for Divl. Batt. at Acheux | |
| | " 2 | | | |
| | " 3 | | | |
| | " 4 | | | |
| | " 5 | | Weekly report to A.D.M.S. Steps laid on water supply. Disposal of manure to dumps selected & Town Majors of villages. Issue Parade of all San. Sect. at H.Q. at Acheux. Pay re & gas helmet practice. Parade now more on a Sundays regularly. | |
| | " 6 | | | |
| | " 7 | | | |
| | " 8 | | Routine village inspections. Preparation of diagrams of incinerators latrines, urine pits etc for circulation to M.O.s. Manifolder copies made. | |
| | " 9 | | | |
| | " 10 | | | |
| | " 11 | | Routine village inspection. Weekly Sanitary Report. | |
| | " 12 | | Incinerators provided now in all villages notify built 8 & 16 Man. Sectn. | |
| | " 13 | | Draw up Salvage Scheme in case of an advance, & request of | |
| | " 14 | | A.A. & Q.M.G. 29th Division | |
| | " 15 | | | |
| | " 16 | | | C.H.G. |
| | " 17 | | | |
| | " 18 | | | |
| | " 19 | | | |

# WAR DIARY or INTELLIGENCE SUMMARY

Army Form C. 2118

/6th Sanitary Section

*(Erase heading not required.)*

Instructions regarding War Diaries and Intelligence Summaries are contained in F.S. Regs., Part II. and the Staff Manual respectively. Title Pages will be prepared in manuscript.

| Place | Date | Hour | Summary of Events and Information | Remarks and references to Appendices |
|---|---|---|---|---|
| Acheux, Somme, France | 20.5.16 | | Notified of Enteric Case in 29th D.A.C. at Acheux. Investigated & shewed spectr. for possible similar earlier cases. Spent parade, Sanitary practice shop, & R.O.s re. | Copy of Sanitary orders & diagram attached |
| | 21.5.16 | | Further visit Acheux. Sanitary orders prepared & issued. | |
| | 22.5.16 | | Routine village inspections | |
| | | | Visit Acheux with French Military M.O. V/c district re. sanitary private latrines. Temporarily unfit to Sanitary Work while from Div & Rest at their 2nd to Equilibria. Town Major. | |
| | 27.5.16 | | 1st Monthly Sanitary Report to D.D.M.S. sent to A.D.M.S. (interviewed) 2 half days next in personal charge | |
| | 28.5.16 29.5.16 | | Route Sanitary Inspections | |
| | 30.5.16 | | Attend Conference of Sanitary Officers at Marieux with DADMS VIIIth Corps (HQ. VIIIth Corps) | |
| | 31.5.16 | | Apply Special leave in France | |

L.H.S.

COMMITTEE FOR THE
MEDICAL HISTORY OF THE WAR
Date   -5 OCT. 1916

# WAR DIARY of 1/1st Sanitary Section 2nd Division

## INTELLIGENCE SUMMARY

Army Form C. 2118

(Erase heading not required.)

| Place | Date | Hour | Summary of Events and Information | Remarks and references to Appendices |
|---|---|---|---|---|
| Albert Somme | 6.6.16 | | Visited Mailly Maillet — routine inspection | |
| | | | P.B. men asked for from Base have been supplied & are reinforced by Temp: employment Dis. Reinf. Sgts. & men. Dis. Reinf. from units as unfit for field life. | |
| France | 7.6.16 | | Routine sanitary inspection of villages | |
| | 10.6.16 11.6.16 12.6.16 | | P.B., T.U. & men from units were formed into the 29th & Div. Reserve (a) placed under command (b) distributed in villages of area — abt. 300 men yet to arrive, [illegible] for Ypres. | [illegible] |
| | 13.6.16 | | Leave stopped. Preparations for an advance [illegible] | |
| | 14.6.16 | | Mailly Maillet handed over to 4th Div. All sanitary kept to [illegible] | |
| | 15.6.16 16.6.16 17.6.16 | | Routine sanitary inspections " " " Lectures on Frost and Sunstroke at the Divisional School | |
| | 18.6.16 to | | Routine sanitary inspection | |
| | 24.6.16 | | 2" Div. Reserve (ex Inspecting Co.) Temp. staff armed for sanitary units and repairs. Special fatigue. Staff of Co. abt. 300 O.R. not 10 N.C.O's & men as Standing Orders for S. Coys. War from Brigades. | |

# WAR DIARY
## or ~~INTELLIGENCE SUMMARY~~
### J.16 "Sanitary Section," 29th Division

Army Form C. 2118

*(Erase heading not required.)*

Instructions regarding War Diaries and Intelligence Summaries are contained in F. S. Regs., Part II. and the Staff Manual respectively. Title Pages will be prepared in manuscript.

| Place | Date | Hour | Summary of Events and Information | Remarks and references to Appendices |
|---|---|---|---|---|
| Acheux Somme France | 25.6.16 | | Two cases of Scarlatina Sc. notified on 23.6.16 were traced to billet 21 & 22 in Mailly-Maillet. No evidence of infection in billets, contacts no sign of any apparent list of prevalence. Men to proceed with draw from front area. Route inspections Authuille, Thurlus | Monthly Report attached |
| | 26.6.16 | | | A Sample Report filled with report to D.A.C. Inspector no attached |
| | 27.6.16 | | Monthly report to D.D.M.S. sent to A.D.M.S. Forestilled Sanitatis lecture at Divisional School, 2 we sent to Conference of C.O's F. Ambulance at ADMS attended | |
| | 28.6.16 | | 2 me cert of syphilis latistied & Bill, (or killed, one wounded wifed) + sent to Sect to Care dep. | |
| | 29.6.16 | | Spent morning in Aveluy + Mouquet Acheux. Routes inspection St. Dent | |
| | 30.6.16 | | 29th Dis 2 Reserve as we refray road along about the advance is to take place (Roter Row) | |
| | | | Genl Munit also met | |

# WAR DIARY or INTELLIGENCE SUMMARY

Army Form C. 2118

*(Erase heading not required.)*

Instructions regarding War Diaries and Intelligence Summaries are contained in F.S. Regs., Part II. and the Staff Manual respectively. Title Pages will be prepared in manuscript.

16 January 1916 Section 2/1st Devon

| Place | Date | Hour | Summary of Events and Information | Remarks and references to Appendices |
|---|---|---|---|---|
| Achiet Somme | 1.7.16 | | Day of Attack on Ancre & Somme. Was ordered to report to 87 F. Ambulance at Rondecourt. Visited from 11.30 am to 3.30 am 2.7.16. Dairy refuges & convoy wounded from Bapaume to Corp. Cllty Stn at Acheux. | |
| France | 2.7.16 | | C.O. Sam. Sectn & 24 men of Sam. Sectn ordered to Albaune. Rmorz. Sn? Ambulance arrived 11.30 a.f. & infm? continuing until 10.0 am on 3rd. Staff Sgt. Sand & 1/c Aukny recv'd Exceptional conduct in recovering wounded under fire in "No Man's Land" 2 men of Sam. Sectn wounded on 2nd & little stretcher bearing. Routine Sanitary duties. Weekly Sanitary report sent in late. | |
| | 3.7.16 | | Visited Auchonvillers, Mailly & Sylleleu. Btn. Routine sanitary inspection | |
| | 4.7.16 | | | |
| | 5.7.16 | | Visited new section of line at Hamel & arranged with C.O. the wants conduct attached to S. Sectn Men cleared dirt latrines pat drained puddles & inspected villag. of Hamel. Very heavy shelling & lachrymatory gas shell. Visited Sylleleu, Mesnil & Mailly Maillet | |
| | 6.7.16 | | Visited Argiens. Whole area is now very dirty & sanitary neglected during recent fifty | |
| | 7.7.16 | | S.Senior of Sanitary Cherp of Sectn personal & chief officers Routine inspection. Visited town council & hadad Sanitary court & headed Sanitary neigh Riris — Town Major to 4 Divs. to rectify Sanitary sectn. Well looked | |
| | 8.7.16 | | Mesnil & Mahrel. Gave over Command of Sectn to Capt. J. Crawford R.A.M.C. | |

July/16 • Sanitary Section • 16 • R.A.M.C.T.
I 29 Div.

**WAR DIARY**
or
**INTELLIGENCE SUMMARY.**
(Erase heading not required.)

Army Form C. 2118.

| Hour, Date, Place | Summary of Events and Information | Remarks and references to Appendices |
|---|---|---|
| 9/7/16 Acheux | Resumed Command of Section after being invalided for a while and afterwards detained doing duty as M.O. in No 10 General Hospital, Rouen. Visited the whole district with Capt Snell R.A.M.C. and took over from him | |
| 10.7.16 | Visited Englebelmer and wrote adjacent for billeting of troops, sanitation of trenches, and made arrangements. Made arrangements. Visits Mailly Wood Camp, saw Cmdt and made similar arrangements. Visits Acheux sources re water supp, and disposal of filth, water, L/Cpl Snell with detl 7 men Personnel R/cpl "BERRILL" No 1, L/Cpl Snell with detl 7 men for promotion to a/Corpl with pay to be made Substantive to complete establishment. | |
| 11.7.16 | Routine visits, Englebelmer, Acheux. Engelbelmer heard Auzières Sunday supervision. "No much can be done of people. | |
| 12.7.16 | Visited Section. St Graelin and found things fairly satis. Left Section Pte P. Cockell Camp nrs Acheux wood, General Supervision Pte P. Heaton and Cash reported as reinforce- ments from No 1 Territorial Base Rouen. | |
| 13.7.16 | Saw A.D.M.S. and C.R.E. reference to Sucrerie water supply. CR[E] Saw the tunls put up found refining elimination necessary, and Report O.C. 12 Mobile lab. Bourlon Supplies Certain defective filled in Acheux, Suspecté Acheux horse court, Saw C.O.31 and O/C D Batt Weymouth R.H.A. Routine. | |
| 14.7.16 | Visits Englebelmer, Auzières & Beaumont re new hrs Lavy | |
| 15.7.16 | Inspects horse lines Acheux. Written Report new feathers for parade in afternoon | |

Army Form C. 2118.

January 1916 Rouen T 2g Bn

# WAR DIARY
or
## INTELLIGENCE SUMMARY.
(Erase heading not required.)

| Hour, Date, Place | Summary of Events and Information | Remarks and references to Appendices |
|---|---|---|
| Acheux 16.7.16 17.7.16 | Visited Maily Court. Attended a Sanitary Conference at Marieux under D.A.D.M.S. 5th Army. Scouts went off 'Return Row' (at P.N.d) left very early and bivouacking overnight, during the day, and returned (at completion, which Army) and celebration. | |
| 18.7.16 | Arrived O.C. 12 pack. Saf. pack monkey of Archeux took over. M. how Loutels. Bundles for hill followed from Acheux town | |
| 19.7.16 | Visited Styletown. Market next night train & parties and Similar Afternoon to his Royal Freelance Argent and | |
| 20.7.16 | Anent choirmaster Lebig at Marieul falls. A.A. D.M.G. and Cmdmr ? Acheux called to direct all & helping Rath and arguments by to book. Visited Befhume, Law Stokes / the Guards with Col R. Barnes Camps differed with Duff ? buckle, hearing receive of the Cus trimming to Refs | |
| 21.7.16 22.7.16 23.7.16 | Satisfy fadlie - much thanks expended days. Recalled to sea S/Hdcled billeted at Hautfeld sept-Henryment, cheaper to move. Handed four-release houses, broken to cavalry to the Different | |
| 24.7.16 | 9th Btn. O.M. St. as ever. Will make tour with Sandon officer | |
| 25 Bus. July to be releasing men employed in town thereof | |
| 25.-7.16 29.7.16 | Envoys northern to Poperinge via Beauval. S-ft Hantsbroke Wounded — in ambulance. | |
| Poperinghe 29.7.16 | Billetted at Ecoles, Proven Road, Prev thereon and by Capt. Jacobs Amt. 9 Inf. Bn. 8, 6th Div. | |

# WAR DIARY or INTELLIGENCE SUMMARY.

Army Form C. 2118.

Jan/16 Jan Dec 16 Rome 7.
29 div

(Erase heading not required.)

Instructions regarding War Diaries and Intelligence Summaries are contained in F.S. Regs., Part II. and the Staff Manual respectively. Title pages will be prepared in manuscript.

| Hour, Date, Place | Summary of Events and Information | Remarks and references to Appendices |
|---|---|---|
| POPERINGHE July 30. 16 July 31. 16 | Being shown round by Capt Jacobs of 6 Siege Bee. Visited Ypres in forenoon. Saw four Major and arranged 6 loads of ray ammo tomorrow to be returned from field Ordnance store. Inspected Pians. Found Ypres to be in worse a good condition. A few months. I noticed being about 1 round. No attempt to remedy or damage at all, with the area Difficulty is that many of shell-fire. the sources from Were owing to shell-fire - 6 to 8147. July, nondais Dec - 6 to 8147. | John Rawton Capt Dec 16 Con |

16th San Section

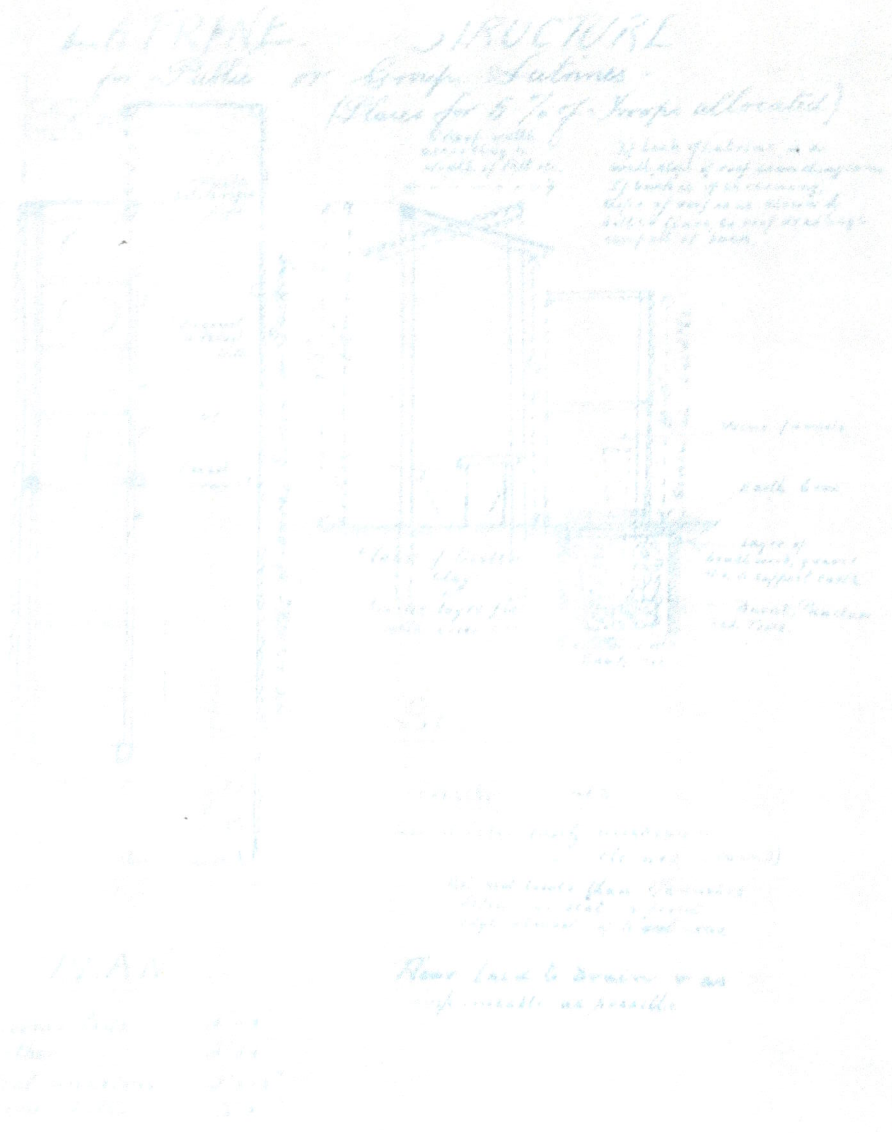


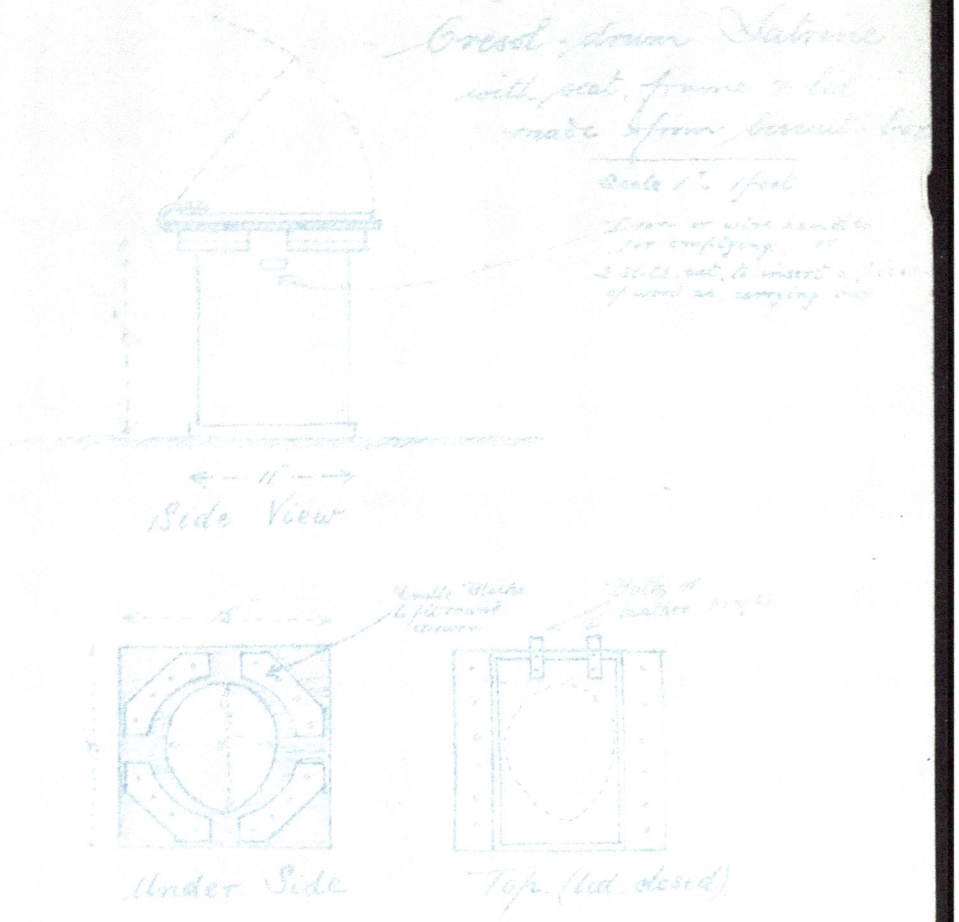


L Hardie Sgt CH
OC 16 San Sect

16th San. Sectⁿ

## LATRINE & URINE PIT
(a) enclosed against flies
(b) with natural ventilation at Schots furniture

### PLAN

### CROSS SECTION

### LONG.ᵈˡ SECTION

### DETAILS
Scale, 1 inch equals 1 foot.

**MATERIALS**

| Shelter | Latrine |
|---|---|
| 2"×2" timber for framework | 2 gal. petrol tins |
| Roof felt | Biscuit-box wood |
| Screening of canvas or sacking | Cases, jam or meat (for urine trough) |
| Bricks, or other flooring | Nails |
| Nails | |

### SECTION   PLAN
Scale: 1" = 1 foot.

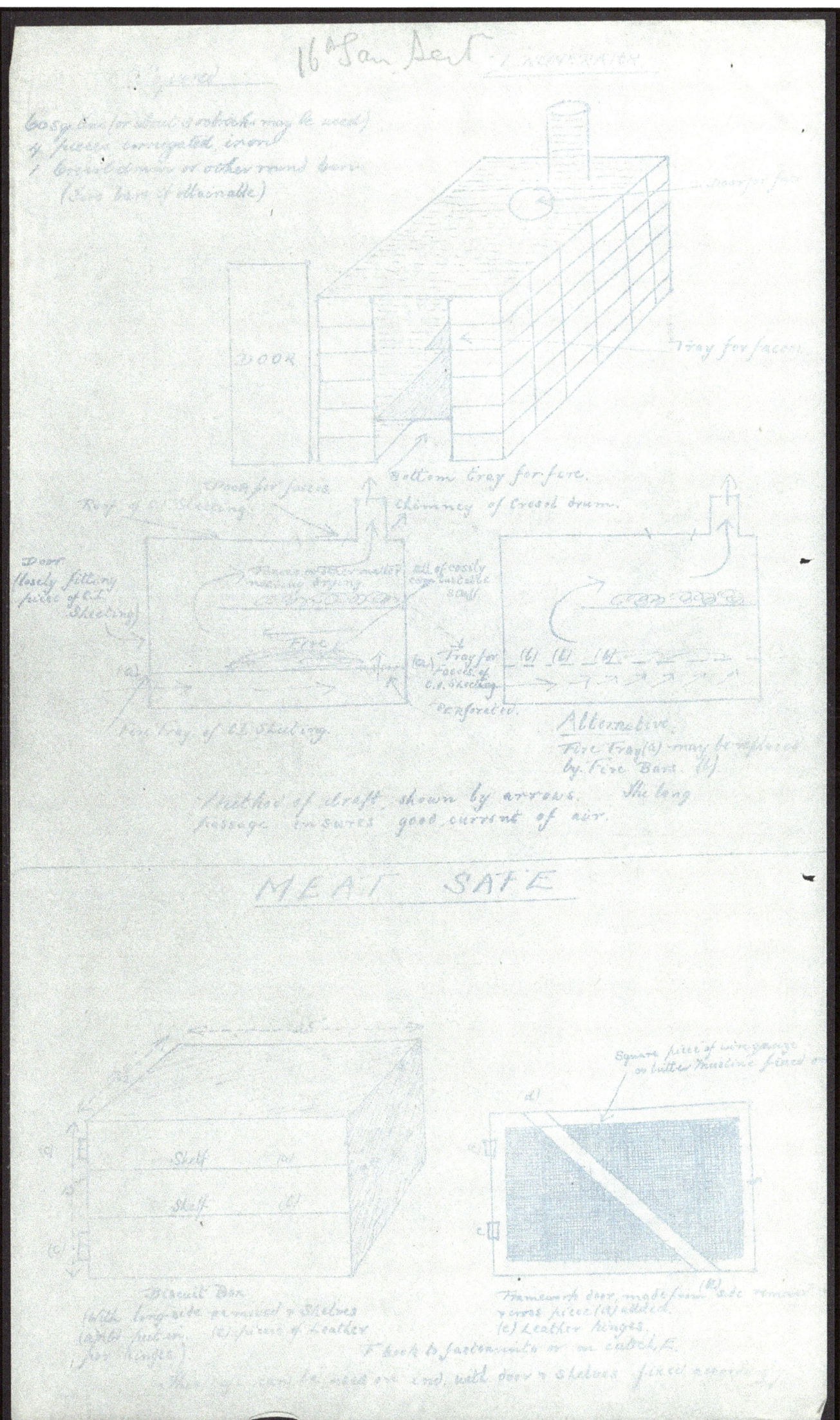

16th Jan Sect

# Grease Trap for Kitchen Sullage

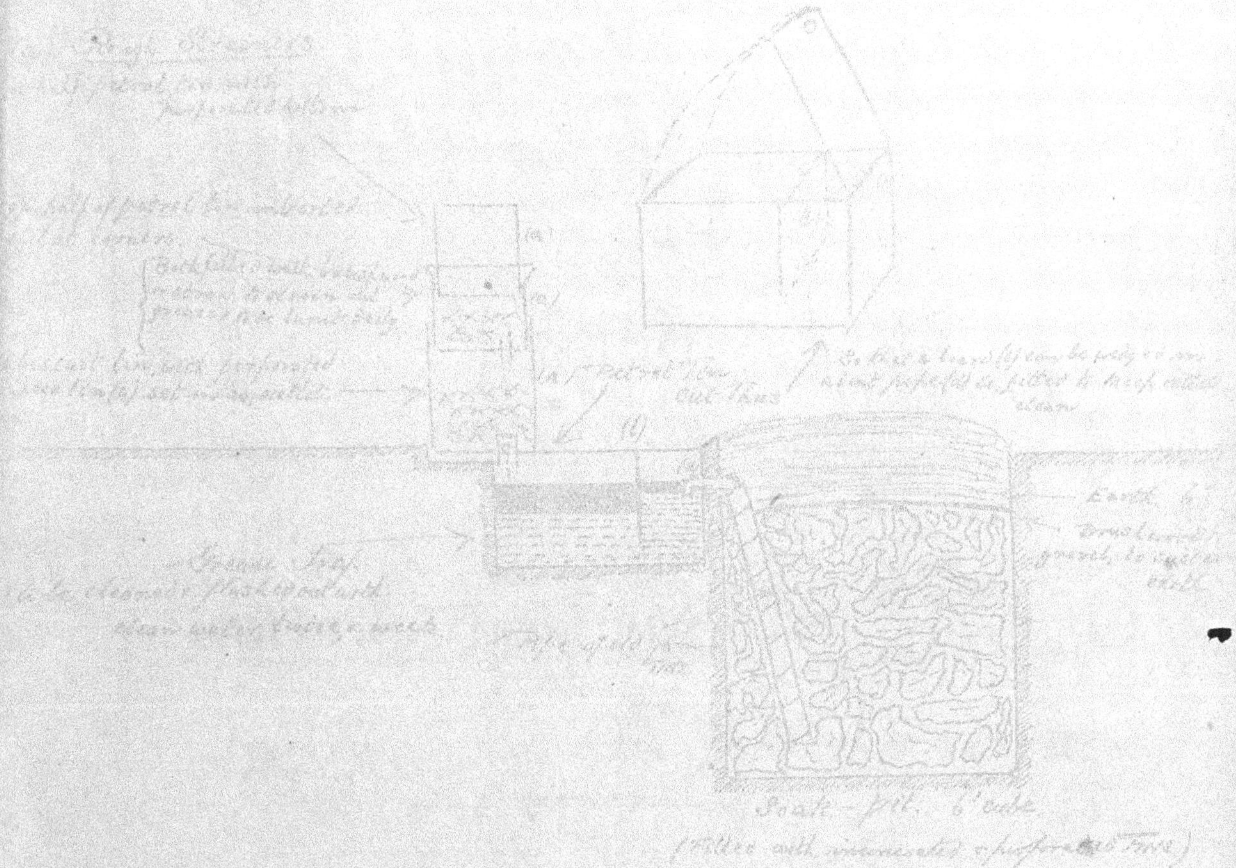

16th San. Sect.

*[Page contains faded hand-drawn engineering sketches of a grease trap and soak-pit system for kitchen sullage, and a strainer for waste from ablution benches with associated soak pit. Most annotations are too faint to transcribe reliably.]*

Legible fragments:

- "a 4" petrol tin cut thus"
- "Grease Trap — to be cleaned & flushed out with sea water twice a week"
- "Soak-pit 6' cube (filled with incinerated & perforated tins)"
- "Earth 6""
- "Strainer for waste from Ablution benches"
- "4" biscuit tin filled with brushwood or straw which must be emptied & burnt & incinerator twice once a day"
- "Pipes of old jam tins perforated (bid?)"
- "Earth 6""
- "Drainage water"
- "Wash Benches"
- "Floor Drains"
- "INCINERATED and PERFORATED"
- "Soak Pit"

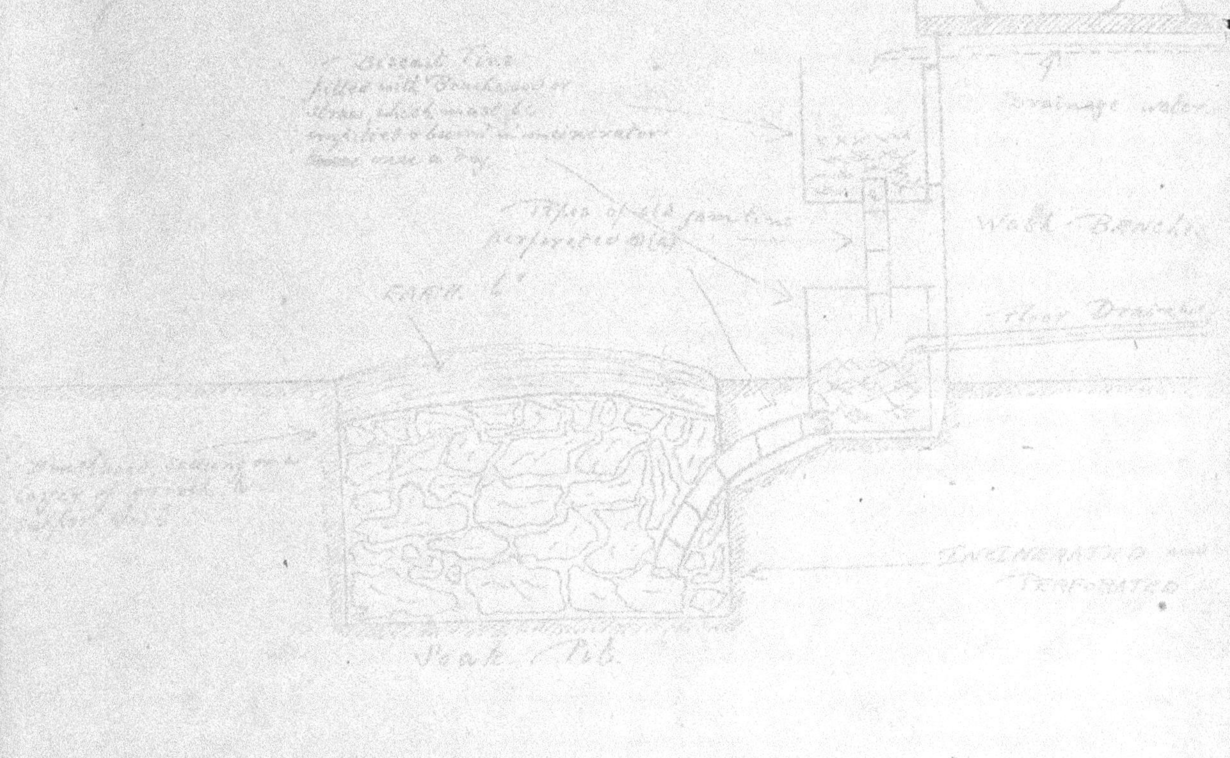

Confidential.

# War Diary
## of
## O.C. 16th Sanitary Section
## R.A.M.C. T.F.

from 1st to 31st August 1916.

( Volume 25. )

Sueee 16 Ranct.

**WAR DIARY**
or
**INTELLIGENCE SUMMARY.**

Army Form C. 2118.

August 1916

(Erase heading not required.)

Instructions regarding War Diaries and Intelligence Summaries are contained in F. S. Regs., Part II and the Staff Manual respectively. Title pages will be prepared in manuscript.

| Hour, Date, Place | Summary of Events and Information | Remarks and references to Appendices |
|---|---|---|
| POPERINGHE. Aug 1. 1916. | Left Off 4 went to YPRES at 9 am & Ypres. Had cart call at 9.30am. Informed by the Div Arrange for Enlarge incinerators for Pow Road school at C camp. Inspected Rounds officers Poperinghe and visited Town Major, and arranged for Lumber for repair to the supplies hire and 6 men I reserve Company. | During this time our officers continued work, latrines, incinerators, incinerators, etc, all from Pop camps, except a Squad at Ypres. |
| Aug 2. 1916. | Inspected steam at 2 pm. had Lt-Col Barnes 2nd Army Toulouges at 2 pm. Had Lt-Col Barnes to some 2nd Army visited Lethlum Westoutre School, officers platoons from that a similar place has been arranged for at Poperinghe 29 Div. Laundry. Visited Ypres & Rampart's visited C Camp, incinerators from found Ypres lym & Rampart was repaired." O.C. Visited Kensington Bow Saw | |
| Aug 3. | C.R.E re Stuff for 89 positions and latrines Visited Bow School at Ypres. Found most water being drunk Undrained. Condition of water there to be checked. Visited Camps arranged for the water there to be chlorinated A and B so went round with the M.O.S. Park lum. Saw trial batch of quarters for making latrines.    Ept | |
| Aug 5. | Writing Reports. Visited also wells in Poperinghe. Lecture tide. Altrades Arms. | |
| Aug 6. | Left for Ypres 6.40 am. met Lt. Col Barnes and with him visited round supplies and Canal Bank. Same arrange went late made for Chlorinating Received on the Cup G'sted (for Army) dispersal of General Visited Ypres again and saw L/C to Rising R.E. who took over water Inspected in Poperinghe | |
| Aug 7. | | C |

San sec 76 Ranic 7
Aug 1916

# WAR DIARY
## INTELLIGENCE SUMMARY
(Erase heading not required.)

Army Form C. 2118.

| Hour, Date, Place | Summary of Events and Information | Remarks and references to Appendices |
|---|---|---|
| POPERINGHE. | | |
| Aug 9. | Went to Vlamertinghe. Saw O.C. to Nohing R.E. as to Chlorination at Ypres. Saw H.Q. of B camp. Arrangements with Camp A.S.C. count for billet for 8 men, then Arrangements at Gas School and Baup School completed. Went to get boxes for latrine at Supply dump, none available. Asked to billet and ration a working party of R.E. detail for well boring. 1 Reinforcement arrived. | Personnel hoped in inspection and exhibition both all over town area |
| Aug 10. | 7.30 Went to Junipert Supply Dump. Sent more proclamation if further needed. Circulars arranged with O.C. W. Riding RE as to Chlorination of water will be commenced when R.E. Supply the necessary tanks. Visited various Camps. Saw about not | One squad at Ypres one square at C Camp a new |
| Aug 11. | Visited Toumlingen, Poperinghe. Visited Inspection Water Road and Peeblock and Hannebeck and went round with D.D.O. Made what arrangements possible. Then left for C Camp. When will see that no refine for inspection of Camp area. Report for actions. | Then new circulars will obstruck under an N.C.O. and 2 or 3 men as required. Busy helping |
| Aug 12. | Visited Peelhoch, Remi, C, O, B, and A Camps with O.C. of squad. Various small disciplines | into Poperinghe Latrines, making Latrines, helping main drains |
| Aug 13. | Visited Ypres head men's Rampants with O.C. A.D.S. Saw A.D.M.S. Afternoon unduly up dairy for march. A sub received stating that no divisions have been sent in. Replied all sent hence from 3/15 except 1 sand cart when O.C. this Section went sick at Marseilles. Sent in diary for Mar 1 - 26 /16. | |
| Aug 14 | Went to Ypres and visited R. Reeb of trenches. Took a sample Ypres from well at outpost "Railway Wood". Surface water nested 11 yards. Required 2 feet chloride. Laiterie Cleaned by our men | (J.) |

Army Form C. 2118.

Sanitation M. Rainer
Aug 1916

# WAR DIARY
or
# INTELLIGENCE SUMMARY.
(Erase heading not required.)

Vol III

Instructions regarding War Diaries and Intelligence Summaries are contained in F. S. Regs., Part II. and the Staff Manual respectively. Title pages will be prepared in manuscript.

| Hour, Date, Place | Summary of Events and Information | Remarks and references to Appendices |
|---|---|---|
| POPERINGHE Aug. 15. | Attended Town Major Poperinghe. Arranged about mobile incinerator etc. M.O. at A camp. Went to C camp, Trot School and round with M.O. 31st Div. | |
| Aug 16 | Attended "Conference" at D.D.M.S. afternoon. To "Content" and A.D.M.S. 8th Corps. Then to YPRES and Left Vierstraat trenches. Saw M.O. VIII Corps. Saw M.O. of Essex Regt. Samples 1 units from Ramparts. | |
| Aug 17. | Visited D.A.C. camp; talk over Ypres Road and made arrangements. C camp and A camp; sample of water. Saw A.D.M.S. | |
| Aug 18. | Visited G 12 and 47; many units of different Divisions. Went into R.A. H.Q. Vlamertinghe. Saw Staff Officer; went round with C camp san: man. 141 Heavy Battery and Infantry harness C. Camp san. school. Sr units in Elverdinghe Road. In afternoon saw Personnel as before | Personnel as before |
| Aug 19. | men to paid man. Wrote Reports. Q.R.E. men in billet. Went to 47 and saw M.O. trenches near Potter alias Aperleut 88 M.G. Co; about camp. Went into Ypres and to Zillebeke with Sgt. Back to C camp. C.R.E., AA-QMG, and A.D.V.S. | |
| Aug 20. | Saw C.R.E. reference water at Ypres and nuisance at Vlam-ertinghe. Saw M.H. Police re manure, interviewed. 14 Batt and W. Riding R.E. Visited O camp C camp. | |
| Aug 21 | Went to C camp 8.45 fixed up men; made Ypres; called at 26 B2S HQ. To see Staff Captain ask re pumping parties for water, Chlorination. Went with Lt-Jean and Trinder of S.W. Borders. Saw M.O. In afternoon to Watten and Reuilkerque, 24th Div. | |
| Aug 22. | Wrote there. Went to C camp. Thru Ypres through arranged for Chlorination of wells at Reutgarde. Went to Nevelmerch, interviewed O.C. 4 Mobile Laboratory as to soap effluents. | |

Number 16 Point 7.
Aug 1916

# WAR DIARY
## INTELLIGENCE SUMMARY
*(Erase heading not required.)*

Army Form C. 2118.

| Hour, Date, Place | Summary of Events and Information | Remarks and references to Appendices |
|---|---|---|
| POPERINGHE Aug 23. | Spent all morning awaywards with offices and made arrangements with offices and Q.M. Sgts. Called at C Camp. O. camp. & saw no. 1 there. Experiments in scoops effective. | (Personnel) |
| Aug 24 | Went to Ypres. Saw Stoff Captain referenced looked at Railway Hill Crates at MHP. reported at 14. C. 16. Inspected Chimneys. L.O.C. 88 F.A. 741 Batty. Ylameretage and had a report from L.O.C. 88 F.A. 2D despatory arrived to A. Camp, C camp. D.C.M. awarded Staff Sgt Lord for meritorious conduct on July 2. (DRO no 290 Aug 24/16 | Nature and type described. See below. |
| Aug 25. | Attended at 4. P.M about some Siems Maj Grey, 9.5.0. about Nature of siege School, water Capt Great Cogan, Saw Agt. C.R.E. and drove out withdrew from C camp inspected what was necessary. He promised to get enough the work of our model lectures he has reported much repts. and saw was necessary. to withdraw manfrom Sanctuary timber efforts. Inspected Poperinge & for month. | Ypres — 7 Camps — 12. Huts — 5 Rooms — 3 Poperinghe — 1 Sector H.Q. Gen. HQ. — 6 Special Sub — 1 Attacks on — 2 (Guards) — 4 |
| Aug 26. | Went to Ypres. went round with O.C. A.D.S. Rampart & Canal Bank. A.D.M.S. handed D.C.M. Ribbon to Sgt. L. | 41 |
| Aug 27. | Went to C Camp. Saw O.C. 88 F.A. from R.E. Saw O.C. 88 F.M. No material yet arrived also seen to hole report in. Monthly monthly report handed in. | |
| Aug 28 | Went to C Camp & Ypres & 30 min refreshments best. to C.R.E. left met by adj. ack. denial etc. for C Camp. Arranged to develop from VIII Corps two from, to lend a Cpl to take charge Spook in Poperinghe. | |

Army Form C. 2118.

Hunbee 16 Reinet

Aug 1916   WAR DIARY
            or
        INTELLIGENCE SUMMARY.
          V
        (Erase heading not required.)

| Hour, Date, Place | Summary of Events and Information | Remarks and references to Appendices |
|---|---|---|
| POPERINGHE<br>Aug 29. | Took A.D.M.S. officer next to Ypres and O.C. to watch Rehearsal Hazebrouck and a very unsatisfactory state of Ypres road. Suppt. Reunion and took out "Sallypte" Ratisland tad. | |
| Aug 30. | Visited C. camps than O camp with M.O. him to mumurate Pioneer Bath's returning to Vlamit to camps found left in an unsatisfactory state by adjoin. Boden (Ransomstead) took down as to this as it is a practice. Attended return march cause than went to inspect date of Camp A in Las Storm. Found huts tents and wet. | Personnel<br>Return as described |
| Aug 31. | Went to C. camp and from R.E. had bought material provides on inder. Remounts of took hung then by Sin. Ser under Capt. went into Ramartinghe replaced punt tassels arrived Capt. Then as dwelled for the R.E. in field form at Ramartinghe Hill where found 2 very hits on muft accompanied one to annex to the a storm descended which made in afternoon. Evening clear | Capt. personnel |

CONFIDENTIAL

WAR DIARY

OF

SANITARY SECTION 16 R.A.M.C.T.

from Sep. 1. — Sep. 30

1916

volume no. 26.

Sanitary Section No. 2 ANZAC?

Sept. 1916

Army Form C. 2118.

# WAR DIARY
or
# INTELLIGENCE SUMMARY.
(Erase heading not required.)

| Hour, Date, Place | Summary of Events and Information | Remarks and references to Appendices |
|---|---|---|
| POPERINGHE Sept. 1. | Visited C. Camp, Pevenleyhrs. Went from there to Ypres. Then saw N.O.S. Inverness Ranks & there. Hunted field latrine for pay for men. Out to A7 & inspected Camp sept by B91 X X SW u | Personnel engaged in routine work N.S. & inspection & construction. Thus — |
| Sept. 2. | Inspected then to Abominic. Paid men there. Went out with M.O. to C. camp & Ypres. Visited N/work and Ecole billets. Wrote memo re home. Weekly Report to A.D.M.S. | Ypres — 7 |
| Sept. 3. | Visited S.O. Poperinghe are employed 1 NCO & 9 Men destined to C. Camp and Ypres. Took men for relief there. Inspected all transport lines, R.S.O., 2 DAC Hors in Ypres Road and A Camp. | Camps — 12 middle area 4 |
| Sept. 5. Sept 6 | L/Cpl Kralen billeted with Sonnenberg Poperinghe for duty there. Visited "½" Munitroh Pimie Bath. A.D.M.S. Bom Workshops, and C. Camps. D.A.C. tents and Tel lines, Bordn Reg. Detailed L/Cpl Stewart to report each Chervolin & write in Bath area. | Rear area — 4 Isolated 2 Special wk 2 H.Q. Lottrine 6 |
| Sept. 7 | Visited Ypres. Wk OC, A.D.S. to Ypres Canal, Ypres Canal. Ran Ramparts. Inspected Incineratic with Town Major & advised him that there are great advantage & alternate in various grounds. Inspected certain block at Vlam - groups. & Ecole bridge there and at G.12 a. Wrote A.D.M.S. re to this & last. | Attached draws 3 / 40 |
| Sept. 8. | Visited lines of A 92 XX BW on A7 & made arrangements for cleaning up. Visited Wanoupte Chateau saw Staff Capt and made arrangements for Chervolin & leaving attached work there. Visited several units as to disposal of manure. Advised in wet weather and installed latrines the females & toilets where farmers cannot be arranged with. |  |

Sanctuaire. 16 Rame T.

Sep. 1916

# WAR DIARY
## or
## INTELLIGENCE SUMMARY.
*(Erase heading not required.)*

Army Form C. 2118.

| Hour, Date, Place | Summary of Events and Information | Remarks and references to Appendices |
|---|---|---|
| POPERINGHE | | |
| Sep. 9. | Inspected & reported on No.4 Sub Camp left by B 93 and B.A.C. Weekly reports written. | |
| Sep. 10. | Attended Church. Went to C Camp) round with M.O. Inundated. Then on to B Camp and saw A.C.91 XXXIV. Pai Sexton and Green. A.S.C. N.T. Infant two days pay for dinning at excessive speed on 8/9/16. Chaplain to A.P.M. | |
| Sep. 11. | Ypres - C Camp, returned from Canalmouth at C getting billeted. This being done by Sanctuare. Inspected ? detail. applied to R.E. | Personal |
| Sep. 12. | Inspected new Ypres Canal again. Applied Relief of men billets on the street. Ypres Cant also requested a Cpl. 2/3 Coy R.E. and details to draw out and issue filter fires. | were as before |
| Sep. 13. | Visited C Camp Sax Camp A97 and new Artstoken arrangements. Inspected ?. Visited 1/2 Mammoth camp Ghezelestein. Attended ?. Visited at Elverdinghe and H.Q. 7th. 88 B. de. Went to ? the Laundry effected repairs & ?. It all got busy. Inspected baths and Laundry with O.C. 6th. Visited H.Q.D.A.C. of to arrange for meal-rep?. | |
| Sep. 14. | Visited 2q Sub Section with Sgt Reed and made various arrangements. Went to Ypres with Capt Williams. X.O. 38 ? as to baths Chevrolet Kaie. | |
| Sep. 15. | Law no. 17 at F.DS. Visited all 15th B.de Bastione lines. And all D.A.C. ? and had with Brit School. Saw A.D.T. CR ? ? to ?-heating incinerator at C Camp. He promised material. | |

Army Form C. 2118.

Sep. 1916. Fanteux Section 16 Army C.7.
777

# WAR DIARY
or
# INTELLIGENCE SUMMARY.
(Erase heading not required.)

Instructions regarding War Diaries and Intelligence Summaries are contained in F.S. Regs., Part II. and the Staff Manual respectively. Title pages will be prepared in manuscript.

| Hour, Date, Place | Summary of Events and Information | Remarks and references to Appendices |
|---|---|---|
| POPERINGHE | | |
| Sep. 16. | Went to C. Camp and made Returned, wrote weekly reports. Then to Ypres, Reninghelst, and Vlamertinghe, & saw Major and Sgnr. Pitt Yrles. A camp into O.C. Broken Rgt. Inspected wells at C. Camp, and wells samples tested, then R.S.O. Scot. Stevenshock & return. | Routine work & |
| Sep. 17. | 29 Div. Jones Coy. came Sept & R Kulun to 1 D.C. on time and made Information. | Personnel as |
| Sep 18. | Inspected C. Camp and read Ypres: Nothing special seen. Visited dug outs in Yres today. Area interesting. | Accorded |
| Sep. 19. | Attended A.D.M.S. C.R.E. Kuul's Railhead and first workshops, made arrangements for improvements here. | |
| Sep 20. | Went to C. Camp and B. Camp. Made C.R.E. and delay in delivery material for finishing installation at C. Camp. | |
| Sep 21. | Capt. J. Crawford O.C. Sandecub went on special leave. Command taken over by Capt. R. Hulin first Range atts. a. & m.s. | |
| Sep 22 | O.C. visited Ypres, Potijze, Innerkein accumulated at M.L. Tunnelling Coy., Railway, still pushed out to Menin Rd. | |
| Sep 23 | Capt L. B&c. O.C. Visited L. Search trenches, digging room at Menin Rd. Potijze & S. Jean. | |

Sanctuary Section 16 Ranne T.
September 1916

# WAR DIARY
## or
## INTELLIGENCE SUMMARY.

Army Form C. 2118.

| Hour, Date, Place | Summary of Events and Information | Remarks and references to Appendices |
|---|---|---|
| POPERINGHE 1916 | | |
| Sep 24 | O.C. Visited Poperinghe, Hazebrouck, Wormhoudt. | ⎫ Personnel |
| Sep 25 | ⎫ | ⎬ occupied in |
| Sep 26 | ⎬ Routine | ⎭ routine as |
| Sep 27 | ⎭ | described. |
| Sep 28 | | |
| Sep 29 | | |
| Sep 30 | O/C. Visited C Camp & Ypres | |

JmLenfn Cap' Rouet

29 N. Div.

140/172

16th Sanitary Section.

Oct 1916

COMMITTEE FOR THE
MEDICAL HISTORY OF THE WAR
Date -2 DEC. 1916

CONFIDENTIAL

WAR DIARY

SANITARY SECTION 16
(29th Divn.) R.A.M.C.T.

No 20

Sanctuary Sector 16 Rout C.T.   October 1916   Army Form C. 2118.

# WAR DIARY
## or
## INTELLIGENCE SUMMARY.
*(Erase heading not required.)*

Instructions regarding War Diaries and Intelligence Summaries are contained in F.S. Regs., Part II. and the Staff Manual respectively. Title pages will be prepared in manuscript.

| Hour, Date, Place | | Summary of Events and Information | Remarks and references to Appendices |
|---|---|---|---|
| POPERINGHE | 1/10/16 | Capt. T. Crawford returned from leave, reported A.D.M.S. | Routine in district as before. |
| | 2/10/16 | Visited Ypres & Laundry at Poperinghe. Wrote Diary etc. | |
| | 3/10/16 | Saw S.O. 55' Div. reference handing over. Visited A.S.C. workshops. Both A.D.M.S. up to complete each Gradien. 1 Batt. Inspection. | |
| | 4.10.16 | Went to Ypres and made arrangements for relief there. Sent bn at night with relief, bringing back men long absent. Dr. Woods went off in advance party for move in accordance with S.R.O. Accompanied A.O. 55 Div. to Walker Ramparts & Canal. A, B, & C Camps. Hotel etc over. | |
| | 5.10.16 | | |
| | 6.10.16 | Arranged about departure & lorry and fodder transport & wrote A.D.M.S. pointing out latter needed repairs to cab. Self left at Hazebrouck. Horse and man att. to 88 F.A. | |
| | 7.10.16 | Went off at 3.30 a.m. for Proven to entrain. O.C. left with lorry and fodder at 5 a.m. Latter left at Hazebrouck with instructions. Lorry reached Beauval. Self arrived Corbie same night. | |
| CORBIE. | 8.10.16 | Lorry arrived Corbie 11 a.m. Reported A.D.M.S. | |
| | 9.10.16 | Sent out inspecting Iynads to Allonville, Cardonette, Bovand, Vielles Fond Nagy, Corbie and saw A.D.M.S. and A.A.Q.M.G. about carts for cleansing etc. | |

Sanitary Section 16
R.A.M.C.

# WAR DIARY
## or
## INTELLIGENCE SUMMARY.

(Erase heading not required.)

Army Form C. 2118.

Oct. 1916.

| Hour, Date, Place | Summary of Events and Information | Remarks and references to Appendices |
|---|---|---|
| CORBIE 10/10/16 | Orders to move. Cleaning up &c. body forwards after departure of 88 Bde. Billets reported clean. Marched to Ribemont, billeted in mill. | |
| RIBEMONT 11/10/16 | Section engaged principally cleaning up and providing for the Mill. Latrines & incinerators. Saw Town Mayor re Ribemont. | |
| 12/10/16 | Sent out men to visit Bonne & Dernancourt. Nothing needed. | |
| 13.10.16 | Orders for 1 Sgt. & 10 men to go to Bailba at Vivier Mill and there taken over there with 18 men ? Reserve Company to carry on. Town Major ? Bonne and Dernancourt visited after departure of the troops and no complaint found. | |
| 14.10.16 | Visited Fricourt and Fargeual and arranged about the wells & points there. 1 Cpl sent to XV Corps H.Q. | |
| 15.10.16 | Took 4 men & Serving 2 and Fricourt underground and 2 at Fargeual. Visited ½ moonworks, and Vivier mill baths. Reported to A.D.M.S. | |
| 16.10.16 | Visited Baths & supply dumps to obtain Beaching powder where available. Visited Corieup ? 86 and 87 Bde. Found butter Salafarin, saw m.o.s & Sanitary men informers. Saw A.D.M.S. | |

Soubry Section 16
Round 7.

# WAR DIARY
or
# INTELLIGENCE SUMMARY.

Army Form C. 2118.

Oct. 1916

(Erase heading not required.)

| Hour, Date, Place | Summary of Events and Information | Remarks and references to Appendices |
|---|---|---|
| RIBEMONT. 17.10.16. | Left for Fricourt taking men and testing box. Called at Baths. Went on to 86 Bde & left average for Staff Capt. in mistake. Camp. Sent Sgt. and 5 men to 88 F.A. for duty at Camp. | |
| 18.10.16. | On Fort Car removed, no means now available. Say the long distances. Chances of Lorries only. | |
| 19.10.16. | Orders to move to E 11 Central. | During this time 5 men on rota duty at Fricourt and Longueval and a guard of 9 men at Becordel for duty at any Funeral. |
| E 11 Central Camp. 20.10.16. | Visited Squads at Fricourt, Longueval & Becordel. Found Brigades moved into line, Found Baths taken over by 12 Divn. So removed Sgt and men there. New Camp. | Read P/Mr. hut near. |
| 21.10.16 | Cleaning up new Camp. Visited Longueval and walked back inspecting things en route. Found common latrines satisfactory. | Men at E 11 Central cleaning up neighbourhood areas. Lorry very busy. |
| 22.10.16 | Visited Field Cashier and Farriers. | for Canteen officer. |
| 23.10.16 | Visited Battalions of the 88 Bde at Bernafay Wood & neighbourhood. Took all day to get there and back. | |
| 24.10.16 | Becordel. | |
| 25.10.16 | Took Staff Sgt A. Hill and then to Div. HQ. to interview G.O.C. a/c Commission. Volunteered for any medical or line | |
| 26.10.16 | Visited Fricourt. Volunteered for any medical or line. Great work as Sunday work almost impossible under circumstances. | |

Sanitary Section 16
Reserve ??

Army Form C. 2118.

# WAR DIARY
## or
## INTELLIGENCE SUMMARY.

Oct 1916

(Erase heading not required.)

Instructions regarding War Diaries and Intelligence Summaries are contained in F.S. Regs., Part II and the Staff Manual respectively. Title pages will be prepared in manuscript.

| Hour, Date, Place | Summary of Events and Information | Remarks and references to Appendices |
|---|---|---|
| E.11, central 27.10.16 | Wrote monthly Sanitary Report. Sent up a Cpl. and 3 men to Longueval to put up common latrine at Bernafay wood. Rest of unit present. | |
| 28.10.16 | Visited C.R.E. Pommiers and enquired | |
| 29.10.16 | bus and explained various things to him. Left for Corbie at | |
| 30-10 16 | order relieving under-parts. | |
| | 12 noon. arrived 2 pm. then arrived at about 3.30. except those from further parts. | |
| CORBIE 31.10.16 | Saw a.d.m.s. Orders to take over baths. Then try wastegrounds, and D.A.Q.M.G. Sent men to Allonville & Cardonette. Sent men to make contact with Town Majors. Saw Staff and Report. | |

CONFIDENTIAL

WAR DIARY

Sanitary Section 16 R A M C T

November 1916

N° 28

Nov. 1916

Sandenfelsen 16 Army T.

Army Form C. 2118.

# WAR DIARY
or
## INTELLIGENCE SUMMARY.
(Erase heading not required.)

Instructions regarding War Diaries and Intelligence Summaries are contained in F.S. Regs., Part II. and the Staff Manual respectively. Title pages will be prepared in manuscript.

| Hour, Date, Place | Summary of Events and Information | Remarks and references to Appendices |
|---|---|---|
| CORBIE. 1/11/16 | Saw AA&QMG, AD.M.S, ADVS and DADOS reference to working of baths at CORBIE. | Distribution of Personnel as at 10.11.16 |
| 2/11/16 | Saw O.C. Kent R.E. as to baths and went round with his officer, + late talk C.R.E. | NCOs. men |
| 3/11/16 | Went to Mericourt l'Abbaye, Ville, Treux, + Meaulté to report on public latrines here. Structural alterations started at Baths. | CORBIE (T. major) 1   5 |
| 4/11/16 | | VILLE (T. major) 1   5 |
| 5/11/16 | toiling notepaper etc. | |
| 6/11/16 | Saw ADMS. Directed to arrange for putting up latrines at Ville street to visited Town Major there | CORBIE (Baths) |
| 7/11/16 | Saw CRE reference to material for above. Interviewed D.A.D.O.S reference to various things for baths | Caretaker 1   3 |
| 8/11/16 | Arranged to temporarily attach Squads to Town majors at Ville and Corbie for Sanitary work as till incoming Res. w/ 2 men at Mericourt l'Abbaye. | Working baths 2  10 (2 clubs)  clerical 1   1  domestic 1   4 |
| 9/11/16 | Went to Daours, inspected post school & arranged for 2 men to help there for a day or two. Squad left for Ville with some lumber etc. | Lorry Drivers — 2 Toilet ett? |
| 10/11/16 | Visited Ville and Mericourt l'Abbaye. Saw T. majors there. | Daours 7  52 Div. H.Q 1 |
| 11/11/16 | Selzeale at Baths and looked after 3242 men bathed in week and 6262 articles disinfected: Laundry difficult as civilians Eng. | 7  34 |
| 12.11.16 | From to Amiens trying to get clean clothes Authorly obtained and new good socks. Paid men. | Total 41 |
| 13.11.16 | Conference at AQMS. | |
| 14.11.16 | Routine. | |

Sanitary Section 16 Army Corps

Nov. 1916
II

# WAR DIARY
or
# INTELLIGENCE SUMMARY.
(Erase heading not required.)

Army Form C. 2118.

| Hour, Date, Place | | Summary of Events and Information | Remarks and references to Appendices |
|---|---|---|---|
| CORBIE. | 15.11.16 | Went to A2d 97 Cavroy Rd to take over from San Sec 8th Div. Saw Sgt in charge and obtained information onto water ponds &c. | Handed over CORBIE baths to 20th Div S.O. from 12 to 16th 1516 men bathed 8659 articles changed |
| | 16.11.16 | Section moved to A2d97 | |
| A2d97 | 17.11.16. | Went round area with San Sec officer 8 Div. Took over water ponds at Montauban, Carnoy, Talus Boisé and Guillemont. | |
| | 18.11.16 | Visited Carnoy East Camps and drying rooms at Bernafay and sent there a Cpl. and 4 men to take charge. | Personnel 18.11.16 At A2d97 21 " Mtn. HQ 1 " Guillemont water point 2 — 25 |
| | 19.11.16 | Saw DAQMG and received instruction to take over MEAULTE baths. Went to VILLE and arranged for squad there to proceed to | Squads – Corbie 6 Ville 6 2 Lorry drivers 2 2 Foden men 2 — 41 |
| | 20.11.16 | Routine at Carnoy camps. Recalled by wire the squad from Corbie except Sgt. and one man who remain i/c clothes. | |
| | 21.11.16 | Went down to MEAULTE public with men to work the engines there, found baths taken over, but in very dirty and unsatisfactory state | |
| | 22.11.16 | Again at MEAULTE & Corbie with ADMS making arrangements for baths to be placed in charge of Cpl McNicol 1 KOSB | |
| | 23.11.16 | Attended conference at XIV Corps under BGMS 4th Army | |
| | 24.11.16 | Visited Bernafay, Guillemont, Sandez. Inspected water dump and water points & spoke to ADMS 18 Division re former | |
| | 25.11.16 | Saw Camp Commdt (Corbie) as to state of latrines in Carnoy East Camp. Visited new Carnoy water pumps & arranged for chlorination | Men at A2d97 Employed – bath points 7 " drying rooms 5 Construction 3 Inspection 4 Domestic 2 |
| | 26.11.16 | Wrote report weekly & monthly | |
| | 27.11.16 | Visited Guillemont Latrine construction very slow. No labour to be had as unit exhausted. | |
| | 28.11.16 | Saw AQMG re above. S/Sgt San Corps Camp Comdt has RE labour available. Visited MEAULTE | |
| | 29.11.16 | Unwell, did not go out | |
| | 30.11.16 | Visited Bernafay, Trones, Bocquelaine and arranged various detail of Sanitary work | |

CONFIDENTIAL

WAR DIARY

SANITARY SECTION 16
R.A.M.C. T.F.

No. XXII

Sanitary Section 16 Panct WAR DIARY December 1916

Army Form C. 2118.

INTELLIGENCE SUMMARY.

(Erase heading not required.)

| Place | Date | Hour | Summary of Events and Information | Remarks and references to Appendices |
|---|---|---|---|---|
| A2d97 | Dec | | | |
| | 1 | | Visited Baths meaulte. Roulis took 1 Section and distribution as in last report. | |
| | 2. | | "Drying room at Trones Wood and Guillemont. Routine | |
| | 3. | | Weekly reports etc. | |
| | 4. | | Visited Sindy, A.D.S. arranged for new latrine. Guillemont — wrote CRE reference to provision of latrines at new camp enclosing diagram. | Routine |
| | 5 | | Various Sanitary details. Visited NFLD and ½ Hornmetts. | " |
| | 6 | | Visited Drying rooms, Brigadiers Camps, and Carnoy E. Camps. | " |
| | 7 | | Visited boiler - points. Feels to be made again. | " |
| | 8 | | Saw D.A.D.M.S. XX sw. re arrangements for taking over. | |
| | 9 | | Routine carries on as usual. List of Stores at Drying rooms submitted to D.A.Q.M.G. who replies only Socks to be removed. Inspection | |
| | 10 | | Journals - cabs completed and tabulated return made. | |
| | 11 | | Visited Bernafay drying room. Saw A.D.M.S. about Transport Sgt. receipt for Store at Drying rooms & forwards to D.A.Q.M.G. Phoned S.O. XX as to relief for water-points. He refers to dis not intend relieving Pass. | |

Army Form C. 2118.

**Sanitary Section 16 Army.** **WAR DIARY** **December 1916**
or
**INTELLIGENCE SUMMARY.**
(Erase heading not required.)

| Place | Date | Hour | Summary of Events and Information | Remarks and references to Appendices |
|---|---|---|---|---|
| | Dec | | | |
| A2d97 | 11 | | Sanitary Section Divn taking over. Drying room relieved & new withdrawn from water points. O.C. Sanitary 16 to Corps Rest Stn – dinners. | |
| MEAULTE | 12 | | Section struck tents, loaded G.S. waggons and moved to MEAULTE. Bodies billetted & baggage party with lorry to CORBIE | |
| RIENCOURT | 13 | | Section entrained Edge-hill 2 p.m. proceeded HANGEST. Lorry move from CORBIE at 10 a.m. arriving RIENCOURT 3 p.m. Contact made with 34 San Sec | 17 sec. |
| | 14 | | Stores unloaded & lorry brought Section from HANGEST. Staff Sgt. took over from O.C. 34 San Sec. O.C. 16 San Sec arrived from C.R.S. at 7 p.m. | |
| " | 15 | | Visited PICQUIGNY. Saw Town Major & OPI, CRE. Sent out Squads to MOLIENS-VIDAME (4) and PICQUIGNY (6) for duty there and villages around and inspected. | |
| " | 16 | | Visited MOLIENS, CAMP en AMIENOIS, MONTAGNE, LE MESGE, SOUES, SAISSEVAL, OISSY, LE MESGE. | |
| " | 17 | | " PICQUIGNY, BREILLY, AILLY, CROUY. Saw Town Major and O.C.5 PICQUIGNY (no troops there). Saw No. 3 Coy Sup. Train. PICQUIGNY. | |
| " | 18 | | " HANGEST afternoon. Pte Power, contravening A.R.O. 5 days C.B. ~7 days pay. | |

T/131. Wt. W708-776. 50000. 4/15. Sir J. C. & S.

Sunday Section 16 Reinf T. WAR DIARY December 1916

Army Form C. 2118.

INTELLIGENCE SUMMARY.
(Erase heading not required.)

| Place | Date | Hour | Summary of Events and Information | Remarks and references to Appendices |
|---|---|---|---|---|
| | See | | | |
| RIENCOURT | 19 | | Rode to CAMP EN AMIENOIS, and saw Town Major at MOLIENS. Sgt. and 5 men reported from Ballis | |
| | 20 | | Visited PICQUIGNY saw Town Major, asked for more clearing up. Afternoon with A.D.M.S at MOLIENS. Saw Staff. Capt. and hutted asked for for labour by 88 B.de. | |
| | 21 | | Visited HANGEST arranged with Staff Capt 87 Bde to billet Squad for duty in that area. Sgt. Hudson (admonished) for neglect of duty. | |
| | 22 | | Visited DAOURS. Returned to Brig.t School on "Sanitation" Notification 1, 2nd role waters sent to Town Major & M.O.S. Concerned. Arranged for a squad to billet at FOURDRINOY for work there and SAISSEVAL. | |
| | 23 | | Visited SAISSEVAL FOURDRINOY PICQUIGNY | |
| | 24 | | AILLY went round with Town Major inspecting certain billets & (typhoid) fever. Saw Maire and all particulars. Men has day off. | |
| | 25 | | Writing & collating water report. Saw M.O and O.C. 2 Hants Pgt. ask details at RIENCOURT went round. | |
| | 26 | | | |
| | 27 | | Visited HANGEST and SOUES. Sent in water Report | |

(T)

Army Form C. 2118.

Sanitary Section No Rouen 1 WAR DIARY or INTELLIGENCE SUMMARY. December 1916

(Erase heading not required.)

| Place | Date | Hour | Summary of Events and Information | Remarks and references to Appendices |
|---|---|---|---|---|
| RIENCOURT | Dec 28 | | Visited PICQUIGNY. Inspected baths & disinfector, found the in difficulties re coal supply short and poor. Wrote Sanitary Report. | |
| | 29. | | Visited Supply dump & told Supply Inspector as to keeping travel off mud. baths at MOLIENS. On to RIENCOURT, CAVILLON, saw Lt. McNeal as to disinfector. Coal Supply. On to PICQUIGNY arranged to take return foden van with 89 F.A. Found disinfector and baths stopped for lack of coal. | |
| | 30 | | To PICQUIGNY with ADMS reference plate filled places. Arranged with adj. CRE to get stuff for building new incinerate there. Saw Sgt Rees & gave him instructions. | |
| | 31. | | Writing day. | |

J. M. Eastin Capt
Sanitary

CONFIDENTIAL

WAR DIARY

SANITARY SECTION 16
R.A.M.C.T.

Nº 23.

A.D.M.S. 29th. Division No.R.315/3.
-------------------------------------

A.A. & Q.M.G.,
    29th. Division.
_____

    Herewith War Diary of 16th. Sanitary Section which completes those of the Medical Units for the month of January,

12th. February, 1917.

                              Captain,
                For A.D.M.S. 29th.Division.

San Sec 16 RAMC. **WAR DIARY** January 1917.
or
**INTELLIGENCE SUMMARY.**

Army Form C. 2118.

| Place | Date | Hour | Summary of Events and Information | Remarks and references to Appendices |
|---|---|---|---|---|
| RIENCOURT | Jan 1 | | Visited PICQUIGNY and HANGEST making arrangements for departure of Squads to-morrow. Made following acting appointments without pay. Cpl Blakeley to a/Sgt. Three a/Cpls and six a/L.Cpls. | Men engaged on routine work. |
| | Jan 2 | | Sent the two squads which have been att'd to this section since Mar 3.15 to D.M.S. orders to report to Town major CORBIE. Sent tools and some equipment with them. | in villages in area, as last month. |
| | Jan 3 | | Went to PICQUIGNY. HANGEST collected 40 blankets from 87 F.A. for the Sanitary School to be started at RIENCOURT. | |
| | Jan 4 | | Arranged about above. Visited also PICQUIGNY, HANGEST, VIDAME and AMIENOIS Routine | |
| | Jan 5 | | | |
| | Jan 6 | | School of Sanitary instruction started at RIENCOURT. 2 Coolies daily and men shown round Sanitary Sanitary work available | |
| | Jan 7 | | Routine. Went to MOLIENS-VIDAME and PICQUIGNY to report on huts for G.R.E. | |
| | Jan 8 | | Sanitary School wound up, men returned to units & blankets to F.A. | |
| | Jan 9 | | Orders for move received. Visited Villages making arrangements. Wrote and sent in leaving report on water and sanitation. | |

Army Form C. 2118.

## WAR DIARY or INTELLIGENCE SUMMARY.

San Sec 16 R.A.M.C.T.

Jan 1917.

(Erase heading not required.)

| Place | Date | Hour | Summary of Events and Information | Remarks and references to Appendices |
|---|---|---|---|---|
| RIENCOURT | Jan 10 | | Remainder of Section concentrate at RIENCOURT. Settles up billet allowances "Jal" claim - certificates. | |
| CORBIE | Jan 11 | | Moved to CORBIE, O.C. by lorry, men by train. | |
| | Jan 12 | | Visited forward area, saw O.C. San Sec 34 and made arrangements for taking over. Sgt. and 8 men sent forward to relieve men of 34 S.S. | |
| | Jan 13 | | Making arrangements for transport of stores and men, partly by lorry, partly by Motor section. | |
| A.2.d.9.7. | Jan 16 | | Moved to A.2.d.9.7. and completed taking over from 34 San Sec. | |
| | Jan 17 | | Morning, visited with D.A.D.M.S. BRIQUETERIE baths, drying sheds and bath tents. Saw D.O.R.E. as to San Sec requirements of Camps. Arrange for distribution of personnel. | |
| | Jan 18 | | Visited Camps. Mrs to A.D.M.S. with public latrines and letrine at GUILLEMONT needing attention and asking that R.E. should do work as no men available from San Sec. | |
| | Jan 19 | | Visited BRIQUETERIE. Water points, baths, clothes store, "CARNOY | |

Army Form C. 2118.

San Sec. 16 R.A.M.C. T.

WAR DIARY
or
INTELLIGENCE SUMMARY.

Jan 1917.

(Erase heading not required.)

| Place | Date | Hour | Summary of Events and Information | Remarks and references to Appendices |
|---|---|---|---|---|
| A2.d.9.7. | Jan 20 | | Visited huts, draying rooms, water points, GUILLEMONT and GINCHY. Found latrines at A.D.S. and GUILLEMONT full as stated. Wrote to A.D.M.S. on this, asking that R.E. should do the work. | |
| | Jan 21 | | Visited Camps with D.O.R.E. and saw various people about details. | |
| | Jan 22 | | Routine. | |
| | Jan 23 | | Staff Sgt Laird left unit for England, candidate for Commission. Lecturing at Bn's School, DAOURS | |
| | Jan 24 | | | |
| | Jan 25 | | Visited all Camps and made notes of requirements. Saw D.O.R.E. and Town Major. | |
| | Jan 26 | | O.C. on leave. Unit in charge of D.A.D.M.S. | |
| | Jan 27 | | The question of latrines at GUILLEMONT urgent. 3 men of section sent up to dig but such a small fond, no good every to feet. Nailed up latrine and made a fail on close by. | |
| | Jan 28 | | | |
| | Jan 29 ? | | Routine & half daily rather interfered with by frost. Inspection routine & water lins | |
| | Jan 30 | | Started some construction of Latrines done at HOT Camp. | |
| | Jan 31 | | | |

CONFIDENTIAL

WAR DIARY

SANITARY SECTION 16
R.A.M.C.T.

N° 24

Army Form C. 2118.

Sanitary Section 16 R.A.M.C.T.

# WAR DIARY
or
## INTELLIGENCE SUMMARY.
(Erase heading not required.)

February 1917.

Instructions regarding War Diaries and Intelligence Summaries are contained in F. S. Regs., Part II. and the Staff Manual respectively. Title pages will be prepared in manuscript.

| Place | Date | Hour | Summary of Events and Information | Remarks and references to Appendices |
|---|---|---|---|---|
| CARNOY A2.d.9.7 | Feb 1. | | O.C. on Leave. Section ¼ Capt Panton R.A.M.C. D.A.D.M.S. | Distributed 1.2.'17 Personnel. |
| | Feb 6 Feb 7. | | Routine Sanitary work in Divl. area. Special attention to GUILLEMONT Camp where Cabines in two flats, in spite of previous Letters etc. | General ... NCO 1 new Sleep ... 1 Camps inspect. 2 Latrine ... 4 water carts ... 1 Clothes disinf. ... 1 clean clothes ... 3 domestic ... 1 Gum boots ... 2 Settlement water 2 Corbie ... 1 D.H.Q. ... 1 Div. School ... 1 |
| HEILLY | Feb 8. | | Section moved to HEILLY. Baths taken over by Sgt BLAKELEY | 4 / 20 / 24 |
| | Feb 9 Feb 10 | | Cleaning up baths & billets at HEILLY. | |
| | Feb 11 | | Squad despatched to villages of area thus — RAINEVILLE area — 4 Bussy & DAOURS — 3 MEAULTE — 4. | |
| | Feb 12. | | Inspn visit from Section H.Q. to LA HOUSSOYE, BONNAY, HEILLY. O.C. returns from Leave. Visited RAINEVILLE, COISY, CARDONETTE and saw Town Majors here and NCOs of Squads | |
| | Feb 13. | | Visited MEAULTE saw Town Major. Attended DDMS XIV Corps to ask about area for Sanitary Section. Told no arrangements | |
| | Feb 14 | | Took Pte Healer, as orderly, to Div. School to work baths here. On to Bussy and Raineville. Afternoon to Bonnay. | |

Army Form C. 2118.

# WAR DIARY (2)
## or
## ~~INTELLIGENCE SUMMARY.~~

Sunday Section 16 R.E.M.C.T. February 1917

(Erase heading not required.)

Instructions regarding War Diaries and Intelligence Summaries are contained in F. S. Regs., Part II. and the Staff Manual respectively. Title pages will be prepared in manuscript.

| Place | Date | Hour | Summary of Events and Information | Remarks and references to Appendices |
|---|---|---|---|---|
| MEILLY | Feb 15 | | Morning to MEAULTE, then to MINDEN POST, arranging to take over from O.C. San Sec 34. | |
| | Feb 16 | | Also next day at BRONFAY reporting on baths etc. | |
| | Feb 17 | | To LA NEUVILLE about champagne blankets - not done. Report on area. Squads reported ready for move. Some men very frost bitten. | |
| | Feb 18 | | Received telegram (adj) Thaw precaution, but sent up Sgt and 5 men in Ambulance for immediate reliefs at Combles etc. NCO and 6 men came down from 34 Sandec when place. | |
| | Feb 19 | | Rode over to DAOURS and lectured at Sgt School at 6pm and | |
| | Feb 20 | | 10 am L/Cpl COSBY reprimanded and Pte ASHWORTH 5 days CB for continuing to talk after 2200, and spilt 1 meal. | |
| MINDEN POST | Feb 21 | | O.C. from to MINDEN POST. No way of moving men or stores owing to thaw precaution. Visited BRONFAY Camps. Arranged to bring up NCO and men in Ambulance to relieve men of other Section there. | |
| | Feb 22 | | Visited COMBLES and HAIE WOOD. Reported on food latrines at Culter place. | |
| | Feb 23 | | Visited HARDECOURT and MALTZ HORN camps. | |

Army Form C. 2118.

(3)

Sanitary Section 16    February 1917
Rawet.

WAR DIARY
or
INTELLIGENCE SUMMARY.

(Erase heading not required.)

Instructions regarding War Diaries and Intelligence Summaries are contained in F. S. Regs., Part II. and the Staff Manual respectively. Title pages will be prepared in manuscript.

| Place | Date | Hour | Summary of Events and Information | Remarks and references to Appendices |
|---|---|---|---|---|
| MINDEN POST. | Feb 24 | | Visited & inspected at COMBLES, rearranging duties of men there. | |
| | Feb 25 | | Visited HARDECOURT, sprayed hut where case of cerebro-spinal had been. Sgt Reed brought up remainder of men and stores in lorry and men of other section sent down. | |
| | Feb 26 | | Writing reports. Visited BRONFAY & 108 Camps. | |
| | Feb 27 | | To MEAULTE for money to pay men. | |
| | Feb 28 | | Writing Report and diary. | |

Personnel.  28. 2. 17

|  | NCOs | men |
|---|---|---|
| COMBLES | | 4 |
| HARDECOURT | | 1 |
| BRONFAY | 1 | 3 |
| MINDEN POST | 3 | 8 |
| D.H.Q. | | 1 |
| DIV. SCHOOL | | 2 |
| COR1315 | | 1 |
| | 4 | 20 |
| | | 24 |

Jan Crawford Rennel
Sant Capt 16
Feb 28
Sam/

WAR DIARY

CONFIDENTIAL

SANITARY SECTION

MARCH 1917

N° 25

Sanitary Section 16
R.A.M.C.
I

Army Form C. 2118.

# WAR DIARY
or
# INTELLIGENCE SUMMARY.

March 1917.

(Erase heading not required.)

Instructions regarding War Diaries and Intelligence Summaries are contained in F. S. Regs. Part II. and the Staff Manual respectively. Title pages will be prepared in manuscript.

| Place | Date | Hour | Summary of Events and Information | Remarks and references to Appendices |
|---|---|---|---|---|
| | March | | | |
| MINDEN POST | 1 | | Routine. Distribution of Personnel as last month. | |
| | 2 | | Went to VILLE saw San Sec officer Guards Divn and arranged reliefs Combles & Bronfay | |
| | 3 | | Men relieved at BRONFAY but not COMBLES. Wired San Sec officer Guards Div. | |
| | 4 | | Section moved by lorry to HEILLY. 3 men left at MEAULTE with rats to Town Major there. | |
| HEILLY. | 5 | | Squad sent out to VILLE and from HEILLY to BONNAY, MERICOURT, LA NEUVILLE, LA HOUSSOYE | |
| | 6 | | Squad sent to LA NEUVILLE for Rat and BUSSY. Visited BONNAY, MERICOURT, MEAULTE, VILLE, MERICOURT. | |
| | 7 | | Inspected water supply HEILLY. Afternoon at BUSSY les DAOURS | |
| | 8 | | Reports on 'Javellisation' (water) & water carts. Afternoon LA NEUVILLE. | |
| | 9 | | Morning inspected HEILLY and Divn HQ. Afternoon at MEAULTE, TREUX, MERICOURT where saw M.O. Lanc. Fus. ref. German measles. Several disinfections yesterday & today. | |
| | 10 | | Morning weekly report on Area. Sent in Memo anti infantum conditions at MEAULTE. | |
| | 11. | | Went to MEAULTE saw Town Major; explained incinerator to him. Went round TREUX with Cpl. and afterwards wrote Staff Capt. 86 Bde ref. cleaning parties at TREUX | |
| | 12. | | Sent instructions to Squads to have reports by 15th | |
| | 13. | | Visited MEAULTE saw Town Major and M.O. Nfld Reg. ref Diphtheria. Took 12 Swabs and disinfects 4 billets. Returned Swabs to 38 C.C.S. | |

①

**WAR DIARY** or **INTELLIGENCE SUMMARY.**

Army Form C. 2118.

Sautec 16 Raineet March 1917.

| Place | Date | Hour | Summary of Events and Information | Remarks and references to Appendices |
|---|---|---|---|---|
| HEILLY | 14 | | Went to MEAULTE with men Sunds (24) for NP&T Pay. Made reports on subject to A.D.M.S. | 14/3/17 Distribution as at <br> NCO men <br> HEILLY 2 13 <br> MEAULTE 1 2 <br> LA NEUVILLE 1 1 <br> CORBIE 0 1 <br> DAOURS (Div. Schl) 0 2 <br> D.H.Q. 1 0 <br> 5 10 <br> 24 (1 under strength) |
| | 15 | | Morning to 38 CCS about Dip. Cases. Afternoon at BONNAY. | |
| | 16 | | Morning lectured at Div.l Schl. Afternoon at MEAULTE VILLE and TREUX about infecting Cases. Disinfector ref. to Byd. Sinds. 1 86 M.G.C. | |
| | 17 | | Morning lectures at Div. School. Visited 10 Mobile Lab. | |
| | 18 | | Collected men's kits at Meaulte and Ville and Saw Town Majors there. Finishing flea report. All personnel Collected. Paraded in marching order. | |
| | 19 | | Personnel route march, squad drill, gas respirator inspection. Orders for move. | |
| RIENCOURT | 20 | | Section moved to RIENCOURT by train to AIRAINES, thence march. Lory via AMIENS with O.C. and 4 men | |
| | 21 | | Squads despatches to MOLLIENS VIDAME (88 F.A.) and ALLERY (89 F.A.) Other places infected from RIENCOURT. | (5) |

Sanitary Section 16          March 1917.

Army Form C. 2118.

## III
# WAR DIARY
## or
## INTELLIGENCE SUMMARY.
*(Erase heading not required.)*

Instructions regarding War Diaries and Intelligence Summaries are contained in F. S. Regs., Part II. and the Staff Manual respectively. Title pages will be prepared in manuscript.

| Place | Date | Hour | Summary of Events and Information | Remarks and references to Appendices |
|---|---|---|---|---|
| RIENCOURT | Mar. 22 | | Routine work & inspection. Found area on the whole clean except part of AIRAINES. Stat report on state of Area submitted 25/3/17. No constructional work done. Old latrines usually found intact. | Distribution 22.3.17. |
| | 23 | | | NCOs men |
| | 24 | | | RIENCOURT 2  13 |
| | 25 | | | MOLLIENS 1  2 |
| | 26 | | | AUERY 1  1 |
| | 27 | | | D.H.Q. 1  0 |
| | 28 | | Orders for move. Collecting personnel. Section collected at RIENCOURT. | DAOURS 0  2 |
| | | | Route march and physical drill. | CORBIE 0  1 |
| | | | | 5  19 |
| | | | | 24 (excludes Shaigh) |
| | 29. | | Stati etc. Orders received that unit wd be transferred IV Corps. | |
| VIGNACOURT | 30 | | Unit moved with H.Q. 29 Div to VIGNACOURT. Received orders to proceed to NESLE and join IV Corps reporting to 35 Div there. Reinforcement received a/Cpl. COXON. | |
| | 31 | | Pers run. Stores 3 days rations in preparation for move to NESLE. Have been seen and talked to about his years now. Have begun to know how to work with it. Capt Russell | |

JonCroughton Sanders GR

T/134. Wt. W708-776. 500000. 4/15. Sir J.C. & S.

www.ingramcontent.com/pod-product-compliance
Lightning Source LLC
Chambersburg PA
CBHW081243170426
43191CB00034B/2022